Edward VII

Denis Judd

Edward VII

A PICTORIAL BIOGRAPHY

Denis Judd

Macdonald and Jane's · London

(Frontispiece) Edward as Prince of Wales

To Benjamin

First published in 1975
by Macdonald and Jane's
(Macdonald and Co. (Publishers) Ltd.)
Paulton House, 8 Shepherdess Walk
London N1 7LW

Printed in Great Britain by
Tinling (1973) Ltd., Prescot, Lancs.
(a member of the Oxley Printing Group)

ISBN 0 356 08153 2

Contents

Preface

It is inevitable, and indeed essential, that in a pictorial biography the illustrations should assume a place of paramount importance. All that I have tried to do in the text is to provide the reader with the essence of Edward's life, as well as of the remarkable times in which he lived; the illustrations add the flesh to the modest framework of the text.

In writing the book I have received unruffled support from my publisher Richard Johnson. I also owe a special debt of gratitude to my wife Dorothy, who helped to select and lay-out the illustrations. Picture sources were mainly provided by Popperfoto, with additions from Keystone, Mary Evans Picture Library, and Illustrated London News.

Denis Judd
London, 1974

Chapter One

Queen Victoria's Son, 1841–61

The young Queen Victoria gave birth to her first son on the morning of 9 November 1841. Her sufferings during labour, as she confided to her diary on 2 December 1841, had been 'very severe, and I don't know what I should have done but for the great comfort and support my beloved Albert was to me during the whole time. At last, at 12 m. to 11, I gave birth to a fine, large Boy. . . . It was taken to the Ministers for them to see.'

The Queen and her husband Prince Albert, of the German house of Saxe-Coburg-Gotha, already had one child, Victoria, the Princess Royal, born in 1840 and destined to become (briefly) Empress of Germany, and (more lengthily) the disapproving mother of the Kaiser Wilhelm II. The birth of the baby prince, however, gave the Crown the male heir it needed. On 4 December he was created Prince of Wales, and on 25 January 1842 he was christened Albert Edward by the Archbishop of Canterbury in St George's Chapel at Windsor. Although Victoria's first Prime Minister, Lord Melbourne, would have preferred 'a good English appellation' to the name of Albert, the infant Prince of Wales was hardly the most English of progeny; through his veins flowed the overwhelmingly German blood of the Houses of Hanover and Saxe-Coburg-Gotha, and even in adult life he retained a guttural pronunciation and rolled his r's in a most decided manner. Albert Edward's christening ceremony cost £20,000, his christening cake measured eight feet across, and his godfather, Frederick William IV of Prussia, presented him with the Order of the Black Eagle. These lavish celebrations in part reflected the fact that it had been seventy-nine years since a male heir had been born to the House of Hanover during the reign of the sovereign.

The nation into which the baby prince had been born was the most powerful and the wealthiest in the world. The guns of the ubiquitous Royal Navy, and the irresistible flood of its exports, gave Britain a unique place among the great powers. At home painful and laggardly responses were being made to the widespread demand for political and social reform; during the year of the Prince of Wales's christening there were Chartist riots, while Ashley's Act regulating the employment of women and children in the mines, and Chadwick's report on the 'Sanitary Condition of the Labouring Population', were both symptomatic of social change.

In such brave yet shifting times, Queen Victoria and Prince Albert presented an example of respectable and earnest sobriety which contrasted sharply with the recent hedonistic and frequently ludicrous deportment of the Prince Regent and his raffish brothers. The Queen doted on her handsome, serious and intellectual husband, declaring: 'He seems perfection, I love him more than I can say.' For his part, Albert strove to imbue the British monarchy with a steadfast and respectable purpose so that it could act as a stabilizing and influential force in the life of the nation.

2 Queen Victoria, in the bloom of early middle age, painted by Winterhalter

Central to such an aspiration was a model family life, full of devotion and mutual respect. This the Queen and her Consort triumphantly achieved in their evident and sincere love for each other. It was more difficult, however, to create model children out of their nine offspring. Prince Albert Edward's lot was, in these circumstances, particularly unfortunate. His mother longed 'to see him resemble his angelic dearest father in every respect, both in body and mind'.

For the first seven years of his life, the Prince of Wales (known to the family as Bertie), escaped too strict a regime. Indeed, his first tutor Lady Lyttelton apparently displayed 'maternal tenderness mingled with common sense', and dealt gently with him. Under her tutelage he began to learn languages, of which German, being so commonly spoken at court, came readily to him.

But in 1848 a sharp change in the Prince's education occurred. Prince Albert believed that 'the welfare of the world in these days depended on the good education of princes'; he was, moreover, profoundly influenced by the advice of his confidant, Baron Stockmar. The Baron was determined to give 'a truly moral and a truly English' education to Edward, believing that an abiding love of truth and morality could be forced down his throat. So the unfortunate Prince of Wales embarked on a rigorous and joyless course of instruction. At the age of ten he was working six hours a day, six days a week under an inflexible tutor, Frederick Gibbs. When the Prince was not engaged in academic work, he was required to undertake a demanding regime of physical exercise. Soon Edward was showing signs of depression, which his mother and father at first mistook for a new sobriety of spirit. Above all, his parents felt unable to provide him with the support and approval which he so desperately needed. The Queen and Prince Albert had a low opinion of his intelligence, and his mother openly preferred his elder sister, the precocious Vicky. It was not so much that Edward lacked intelligence, but rather that he lacked intellectual tastes. Despairing of producing an academic high-flier, and fearful that a philistine temperament lurked within the Prince, his father and Stockmar redoubled their efforts to mould his character into an acceptable shape.

Prince Edward's early years were also very isolated. Though surrounded by a host of brothers and sisters, he saw very little of other children. A few hand-picked Etonians came sometimes to have tea with him when he was at Windsor, but he was certainly not allowed unlimited contact with these companions. As a great concession in 1857 he was given permission to undertake a walking tour with four boys from Eton. But almost invariably his parents accompanied him on visits to museums and other places of interest; indeed, when he visited the Great Exhibition his father noted resignedly that he showed an undue and morbid interest in a stand portraying the murderous Thuggees of India.

On his fifteenth birthday (9 November 1856) the Prince was allowed to choose his own food, provided it was a medically sensible choice, and to select his own hats and ties. But he still had no allowance. Controlled as he was by his parents, Edward loved both of them deeply, and 'was pale and trembling' when, for the first time, he took leave of them for several weeks in 1856 in order to study at Osborne, the royal residence in the Isle of Wight. However he feared his father as well as feeling devotion for him, and had to endure the aggressive response of Queen Victoria when she felt thwarted by him. Of course, both the Queen and the Prince Consort needed and enjoyed the company of their children, but could not rid themselves of the desire to regulate their behaviour strictly. When Prince

3 (Above) The handsome and dashing Prince Albert, with whom Victoria fell rapturously and immediately in love

4, 5 The Prince Consort as sober and upright paterfamilias

Edward reached maturity his compulsive conviviality owed much to his earlier isolation, just as his gluttony was probably based on the controlled diet of his childhood.

After 1856, however, his horizons were broadening. In that year he accompanied his parents on the state visit to Napoleon III in Paris, and won French hearts by wearing a kilt. Next year he went to study at Königswinter, near Bonn, where on his first evening he became tipsy and kissed a pretty girl. Later he toured Germany and on one occasion dined with Prince Metternich who treated him to a passionate discourse upon his own diplomatic career, but of whom the somewhat bored Prince merely noted in his diary: 'He is a very nice old gentleman and very like the late Duke of Wellington.'

In 1859 Edward toured Italy, and in 1860 visited Canada and the United States. He was an enormous success in the latter country, and though his mother still fretted over his dull intellect, less prejudiced observers remarked on his charm, vitality and diplomacy. By now he had an allowance of £500 a year, and a modest residence at The White Lodge in Richmond Park. Though he passionately wanted a career in the army his father decided that he should attend Oxford University, but that he should live in Frewin Hall and not amid corrupting undergraduates. It was clear to Prince Albert that at Oxford his son preferred 'good food' to 'mental effort', but Edward did well enough, and was the first sovereign to matriculate from the university since Prince Hal – the future Henry V. While at Oxford he made a number of good friends, as he did later at the universities of Cambridge and Edinburgh; he also enjoyed hunting, cigars and fast company.

As he approached his twentieth year the Prince of Wales was sent to the Curragh Camp near Dublin, since part of the princely programme mapped out for him included some military training. While at the Curragh, his brother officers smuggled an actress, Nellie Clifden, into the Prince's quarters. Later in 1861, when he was back in England, and at Madingley Hall in Cambridge, the rumour of the liaison came to the Prince Consort's ears. Albert hastened to Cambridge to confront his son; Prince Edward adroitly turned aside the paternal wrath by admitting that he had yielded to temptation, but adding that the affair was now over. His father forgave him, while urging him to 'fight a valiant fight. . . . You *must* not, you *dare* not be lost. The consequences for this country, and for the world, would be too dreadful!'

But while staying at Cambridge, Prince Albert, who was over-tired and somewhat depressed, caught a chill, and two weeks later developed typhoid fever. On 14 December 1861 he died at Windsor. Queen Victoria was overwhelmed with grief, and amid her pain insisted irrationally that Prince Edward was responsible for his father's death, telling her daughter Vicky, now Crown Princess of Prussia: 'I doubt if you could bear the sight of one who was the cause; or if you would not feel, as I do, a shudder. Still more, if you saw what little deep feeling about anything there is. . . .' It was in such a mood of anguish and alienation that Queen Victoria began her forty years of widowhood.

6 The devoted royal couple in 1861, the year of Albert's death

7 *Frederick William IV of Prussia, godfather to the infant Prince Albert Edward*

8 *King Leopold I, first King of the Belgians and Victoria's beloved uncle*

9 *Christian IX of Denmark, father of Edward's future bride, Alexandra*

10 *(Opposite) The young Queen Victoria with royal cherubim – the Princess Royal and, asleep, the Prince of Wales*

11 *Prince Albert Edward, Queen Victoria's 'fine, large Boy'*

12 *(Below left) The christening bowl, with water lilies round the lip, used for Edward's baptism in 1842*

13 *(Below right) A sailor-suited Prince of Wales, portrayed by the royal favourite Winterhalter*

14 *(Opposite) The young idyll – Edward with his sister Victoria (centre right) and his brother Alfred (below). The drawing top left is by the Prince Consort, when Edward was five, and was based on an artist's sketch*

KING EDWARD'S EARLY DAYS

15 (Far left) The austere and exacting Baron Stockmar, misguided educator of Edward

16 (Left) Edward in the Highland garb so beloved by the family

17 (Below left) An indolent-looking Edward in young manhood

18 A more studious pose

19 *The French Emperor Napoleon III, at whose court the young Edward wished to remain in 1856*

20 *The French Empress Eugénie, her beauty somewhat faded*

21 *(Right) Together for fourteen years: Albert and Victoria in 1854*

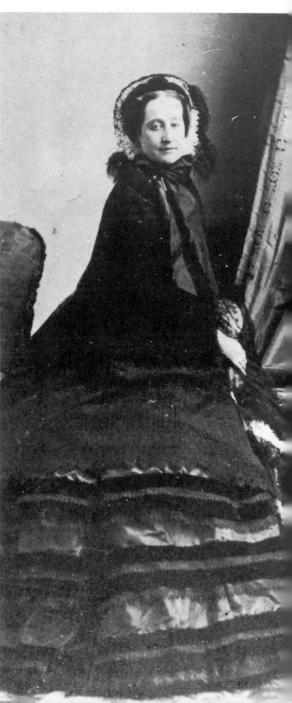

22 (Left) Edward as an Oxford undergraduate. His father noted resignedly that he preferred good food to books

23 (Below) A dispirited-looking Edward surrounded by his tutors at Oxford, including Colonel Bruce (left) and F. W. Gibbs (centre)

24 *(Left) Edward undergoing the military training that was to include his fateful liaison with Nellie Clifden*

25 *(Below) Four royal brothers of the clan Saxe-Coburg-Gotha: Edward with Alfred Duke of Edinburgh, the Duke of Connaught and the Duke of Albany, in 1881*

26 *(Left) Edward and his sister Victoria in gloomy pose*

27 *(Below) Queen Victoria with Edward's bride-to-be Alexandra, in the 'presence' of Prince Albert*

Chapter Two

Family Man and Social Lion, 1861–1901

The repugnance that Queen Victoria felt for her eldest son was slowly, though fitfully, dispelled by the passage of time. Deep and abiding as her grief undoubtedly was, Victoria came to see that Albert Edward's own mourning was heart-felt and profound. She also believed that her duty towards him involved a pious carrying-out of the plans proposed by the Prince Consort before his death. These plans included a tour of the Near East, and an early marriage.

On 29 January 1862 the Prime Minister, the rakish and resolute Lord Palmerston, visited the Queen to discuss the Prince of Wales's future. Palmerston, with his habitual candour, told Victoria 'that the country was fearful we [the Queen and the Prince of Wales] were not on good terms', and he heartily approved of the proposed tour and an early marriage (though he himself had chosen not to marry until the age of fifty-five, and only then to Lady Cowper who had been his mistress for many years).

So on 6 February 1862 in the strictest incognito, and 'low and upset, poor Boy', Prince Edward left for the Near East where he was soon shocking his hosts in Egypt by preferring crocodile shooting on the Nile to looking at 'tumble-down' old temples. The Prince of Wales arrived home on 14 June, having narrowly avoided a lengthy appraisal of Greek antiquities, but causing his mother to believe that 'He [the Prince Consort] would have been so pleased to see him so improved, and looking so bright and healthy. Dear Bertie was most affectionate and the tears came into his eyes when he saw me.' She recorded a little later that 'His time away has done him so much good; he is so improved in every respect, so kind and nice to the younger children, more serious in his ways and views, and most anxious for his marriage.'

Negotiations for the Prince's marriage to Princess Alexandra of Denmark had proceeded during his Near Eastern tour. In September 1862 Queen Victoria, while staying at her uncle Leopold's palace in Belgium, had met the Princess, and wrote in her diary: 'Alexandra is lovely, such a beautiful refined profile, and quiet ladylike manner, which made a most favourable impression.' Almost immediately after this encounter, Edward was enabled to meet and propose to the exquisitely beautiful Danish princess, who straightway accepted him. Edward was enraptured with his bride to be, and assured his mother that 'Love and cherish her you may be sure I will to the end of my life.'

Despite the diplomatic implications of bringing a Danish princess into the royal family when the Schleswig-Holstein dispute between the German states and Denmark was deepening, the marriage was widely popular with the British public. The wedding took place in St George's Chapel, Windsor on 10 March 1863, to the accompaniment of national rejoicing and some indifferent verse by the poet laureate Tennyson:

> Sea King's daughter as happy as fair
> Blissful bride of a blissful heir.

28 *A rakish Prince of Wales puffs one of the cigars to which he was so addicted*

After a short honeymoon, the young couple moved into Marlborough House, which was to be their London home. The Prince of Wales was voted an income of £40,000 a year by Parliament, while Princess Alexandra received £10,000 a year as 'pin money'. These sums, added to revenues from the Duchy of Cornwall and the Sandringham estates, plus the interest from the capital he now inherited from his dead father, meant that the Prince could expect an annual income of between £110,000 and £115,000. This sum, though less than that enjoyed by several hereditary peers (such as the Dukes of Buccleuch, Devonshire and Northumberland), nonetheless gave Edward a flying financial start as a married man. Parliament, however, did not increase his income until his succession in 1901, and there were years when his expenditure exceeded his income by as much as £20,000. Perhaps this was one of the reasons, apart from his taste for cosmopolitan and interesting company, that prompted Edward to develop friendships with successful financial wizards such as the Rothschilds, Maurice Hirsch and Ernest Cassel.

The Prince was deeply in love with his young bride. Alexandra's pristine beauty (which hardly faded until her later years) was combined with a charming simplicity of manner and a warm and spontaneous nature. She was notoriously unpunctual and disorderly (whereas her husband was a stickler for correct dress and etiquette, and always claimed that he knew 'something about arrangements'), and was also an unfailing supporter of charities and good causes, especially nursing. Princess Alexandra bore her husband six children: Prince Albert Victor born in 1864; Prince George (the future King George V) born in 1865; Princess Louise, born in 1867 and declared Princess Royal in 1905; Princess Victoria born in 1868; Princess Maud, born in 1869 and subsequently Queen of Norway; and Prince Alexander John, who was born in 1871 but who only lived for twenty-four hours.

Despite Edward's amorous extra-marital exploits, the Prince and Princess of Wales enjoyed a full and satisfying family life enhanced by mutual affection and esteem. Edward adored his children and was equally adored by them. Determined not to repeat the stultifying parental demands of his own upbringing, he was a relaxed and benevolent father, enjoying robust play – even to the extent of allowing races with pieces of hot buttered toast along the stripes of his trousers. He communicated wonderfully with children of all ages and enjoyed their society. He was also anxious that his children, particularly his sons, should be able to treat him as a friend and a confidant. Though no doubt this was an imperfectly realised ambition, and although Prince George (who became Heir Presumptive on Prince Albert Victor's death in 1892) held his father in some awe, there was unquestionably an enviable rapport between father and children.

Princess Alexandra's relationship with her children was based upon a passionate, simple and sometimes overwhelming mother love. Bolstered by her straightforward belief in Christian virtues, and necessarily somewhat isolated by her husband's intensely active social life, Alexandra clung possessively to her children, perhaps draining them of a certain amount of independence in the process. Certainly Prince George did not emancipate himself from his emotional dependence upon her until he married Princess Mary of Teck in 1893, and even then, as for his siblings, 'Darling Mother-dear' remained a profound influence in his life.

None of the 'Wales' children (as Princess Mary of Teck called them) were particularly cultivated or intellectually adventurous, but then their parents were decidedly philistine themselves. In fact, so dull was Prince Albert Victor (known in the family as 'Eddy'), that he was quickly outpaced in schooling by the bright and lively Prince George. When Prince

Eddy finally succumbed to typhoid in 1892, though his tightly-knit family were sorely grieved by his loss, more detached observers counted it a blessing for the continuing viability of the monarchy that such a backward and slow-witted prince could not now ascend to the throne of the greatest power in the world.

The Prince of Wales, though he had fathered a Victorian family, was not destined to uphold the high, and essentially hypocritical, moral standards of prurient Victorian society. Edward soon transformed Marlborough House into a meeting place for the fastest set in London society. Almost wilfully trampling on the elevated and earnest principles of his dead father, and of his very-much-alive and despairing mother, he plunged into a headlong pursuit of pleasure. He gambled, he attended the music halls, he ate enormously and smoked and drank freely; while Victoria, draped in widow's weeds, shied away from public contact, Edward positively sought it out. He jostled with his fellow-subjects at race meetings, he enjoyed being recognised in the street, he travelled indefatigably, making hedonistic pilgrimages to Paris, to the French Riviera and to the great spas of Europe. It is not surprising that when he finally ascended the throne he was hailed as: 'The monarch to make things hum, The King, the runabout King'.

Queen Victoria viewed these activities with a censorious eye, and wrote gloomily: 'What will become of the poor country if I die? If Bertie succeeds he would ... spend his life in one whirl of amusements.' In 1869 she wrote plainly to her son: 'There is a *very* strong feeling against the luxuriousness and frivolity of society – and everyone comments on my simplicity.' These maternal strictures seem to have had little effect, and the Prince of Wales continued to find the company of Jewish financiers, aristocratic *roués*, actresses and 'professional beauties' extraordinarily stimulating and satisfying.

Given the circles in which increasingly Edward moved, it was inevitable that he should be the subject of rumour and scandal. In 1871 he was involved in a well-publicized divorce case when Sir Charles Mordaunt filed a divorce petition against his young wife, citing two of the Prince's companions as co-respondents. Edward was called as a witness in this case, when he denied (though not all believed him) that he had ever committed adultery with Lady Mordaunt. For several weeks after his appearance in the witness box, the Prince and his wife were occasionally hissed in the streets of London and were once booed when they took their places at the Olympic Theatre. Scurrilous pamphlets appeared, and Gladstone wrote the Prince a cautionary letter reminding him of the unfortunate scandals that had once surrounded the Prince Regent.

Edward's marriage survived this and other scandals – including the arrest of a close friend (Lord Somerset) in a homosexual brothel, the Blandford and Crawford divorce cases, and his involvement in an illegal game of baccarat in which Sir William Gordon-Cumming was caught cheating. His name was linked with a host of delectable women, among them the actress Sarah Bernhardt, Lillie Langtry (the 'Jersey Lily'), Lady Warwick (until she espoused socialism!), Mrs George Keppel and Mrs Agnes Keyser. Nor were his mistresses exclusively upper-crust or home-grown, and it was rumoured that once the Prince was greeted by the voluptuous Moulin-Rouge dancer La Goulue with the words: "*Ullo, Wales, est-ce que tu vas payer mon champagne?*"

Although Edward's escapades provoked criticism from churchmen (particularly Nonconformists), from aristocratic guardians of public morality (like the 'Lambeth Penitents') and from the rumbling editorials of *The Times*, they at least proved that human

Lord Palmerston who, as Prime Minister, urged Edward's
early marriage

31 *Man, and dog, about-town*

33 *Edward in 1863, the year of his marriage*

32 *Still life, with books*

34 *Edward lounging at Osborne*

frailty was not confined to the lower orders of society. The Prince of Wales was able to ride out the 1860s and 1870s when criticism of the monarchy was widespread and republican sentiment had to be taken seriously. Doubtless he was aided by his dramatic recovery from typhoid in 1871 which brought the monarchy some much-needed popularity as well as prompting some unforgettable lines by the poet Alfred Austin:

> *Flash'd from his bed, the electric tidings came,*
> *He is not better; he is much the same.*

By the 1890s, moreover, the monarchy was enjoying the reflected glory of Britain's imperial apogee; indeed, Queen Victoria's Diamond Jubilee of 1897 was a gaudy but stirring demonstration of a global influence that far out-stripped that of the Caesars.

Edward's indiscretions and lavish life-style, therefore, were the more easy to forgive in what were apparently inspiring times. In any case, his wife bore his behaviour patiently, or at least stoically, and his passions for good food, hunting, yachting, horse-racing and light theatrical entertainment were commonplace among the aristocracy of which he was one of the leading figures, and no doubt gave vicarious pleasure to millions of humbler citizens. But popular as he was, Edward was still Prince of Wales in 1900 when he reached the age of fifty-nine, and there were those who argued that his reputation as an ageing rake would ill become the throne.

There was another, more important, doubt as to Edward's suitability to succeed his mother. This lay in his inexperience in matters of statecraft. Far from allowing her eldest son to assume the burdens and responsibilities of the late, lamented Albert, Victoria came to the conclusion that he did not possess sufficient maturity and discretion to be shown state documents or to be let into delicate state secrets. Edward frequently complained, with due cause, that he was kept in complete ignorance of what was going on. As a constitutional monarch his mother did not, in fact, possess any significant political power, though often she strenuously tried to exert influence over her ministers and over events.

Even this, however, was denied to Edward: he was sent on royal tours (to India in 1876 for example), he sat on several commissions, he made a few speeches in the House of Lords, he entertained visiting Heads of State, and met foreign ambassadors at social functions. Not all of these activities were productive of national and international harmony, since he was essentially a conservative in domestic matters and a staunch supporter of imperial expansion overseas. He had a somewhat naïve admiration for men of action (such as Cecil Rhodes), and could display partisan tendencies, as in his strong support of his wife's country, Denmark, against Germany in the Schleswig-Holstein dispute. He was also capable of antagonizing those with whom he came into contact through unguarded statements. In particular, he aroused his assertive and hysterical nephew the Kaiser Wilhelm II to a frenzy of resentment; this resentment sprang partly from the Kaiser's own neurotic sensitivity, and partly from a clash of personalities centring on the relaxed bonhomie of Edward and Wilhelm's strident insecurity.

So, as his mother entered her eighty-first year and the twentieth century began, the elderly Prince of Wales was almost as ignorant of the intricacies of a monarch's day-to-day duties as when his father had died some forty years before. This did not augur well for the future development of the British monarchy, but, in the event, Edward's reign was destined to be full of achievement.

35 *Doleful family group, watched over by the bust of dear, departed Albert*

36–7 *(Right and overleaf) The wedding of Edward and Alexandra, 10 March 1863. Alexandra's father, the King of Denmark, who led a scandalous private life, was not invited*

38 *(Preceding pages) The happy couple*

39 *(Left) Alexandra dressed for the garden*

40 *(Below) Alexandra dressed for the drawing-room*

41 *Alexandra dressed for her favourite parrot*

44

44 (Left) The Princess of Wales with Albert Victor and the baby Prince George (the future King George V)

45 Princess Alexandra (standing centre) with her father and mother, and her sister the Duchess of Fife with her baby daughter

46 *Edward and Alexandra at Cowes for the yachting in 1870*

47 *A still youthful Alexandra and a more rotund Edward*

48 *Edward surrounded by dusky maidens at his landing at Bombay in December 1875 to begin his tour of India*

49 *(Right) The Moulin Rouge, Paris, where Edward made contact with dancers like the notorious La Goulue*

50 *Prince Edward avoiding an irate Indian elephant in 1876*

51 *Edward about to slaughter some Indian game*

52 *(Below right) Alexandra, his first catch*

53 *(Right) The actress Sarah Bernhardt, one of his later quarries*

54 *Sarah Bernhardt in pensive mood*

56 *Peach-skinned Lily Langtry, the 'Jersey Lily'*

55 *Edna May, one of Edward's many 'actress friends'*

57 *A middle-aged Alfred, Duke of Edinburgh, who in 1893 became Duke of Saxe-Coburg-Gotha*

58 *Edward's elder sister Vicky, in mourning for her husband the Kaiser Frederick III, who died of cancer of the throat in 1888*

59 *(Overleaf) Victoria, Edward and Alexandra encapsuled in their finery*

60 *Victorian family portrait. The group includes (from the left) Princess Alexandra and her three daughters, the Crown Prince of Prussia (later the Kaiser Frederick III), Princess Frederick Charles of Hesse, Princess Henry of Battenberg, Queen Victoria, the Duke of Edinburgh, the Prince of Wales, Queen Sophie of Greece and the Crown Princess Victoria of Prussia*

61 *A still from a rare newsreel of the 1890s shows Edward VII (far right) at a Buckingham Palace garden party. His grandson, the future Edward VIII, is seated on the ground with a pet dog*

62 *(Right) Princess Alexandra with her five children, and two dogs. Prince George (far right) is demonstrating his life-long concern for the correct form of dress*

63 *The five Wales children in rakish and nautical mood in* *1874*

64 *(Right) An earlier photograph showing the first four of the Wales children (Albert Victor, George, Louise and Victoria)*

65, 66 *Prince George (the future King George V) aged four, and already in training for his naval career*

67, 68 *Prince George in the uniform of a cadet in the Royal Navy, and with his darling 'Mother-dear', to whom he was particularly close and from whom he hated to be parted*

69 *(Right) Despite Albert Victor's extra inches, Prince George soon outstripped him in education and achievement*

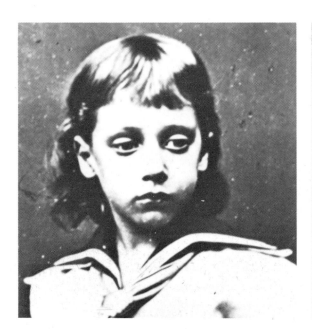

70 Edward's sons as naval cadets

72 (Right) Princess Alexandra looking no older than her three daughters Louise, Victoria and Maud (the future Queen of Norway)

71 The royal Princesses Victoria and Louise of Wales

74 *Edward and his two sons in the early 1880s*

75 *(Overleaf) The Wales family photographed at Marlborough House, their London home. Prince Albert Victor had earlier expressed jealousy over Prince George's fine nautical beard*

72

76 (Left) Prince George as Duke of York, and heir presumptive, following his brother's death from typhoid in 1892

77 The Duchess of Teck photographed in 1870 with her daughter Mary, the future bride of Prince George, and later Queen Mary

78 (Left) The Teck family photographed in 1885

79 The Duchess of Teck and Princess Mary in 1891, the year the latter became engaged to the ill-fated Prince Albert Victor

80 *A radiant Princess Mary (or May) of Teck in her*
'coming-out' gown

81 *Prince George and Princess Mary on their wedding day in 1893, a year after the death of Albert Victor*

82 *(Overleaf) The happy couple and their bridesmaids. Princess Mary found her Wales in-laws decidedly philistine*

83 *Princess Mary with her second son, the future King George VI, born in 1895*

84 *(Above right) Queen Victoria arrives to lay the foundation stone of the Victoria and Albert Museum in 1899, watched by the Prince of Wales, Prince George and other members of her family*

85 *(Below right) The Prince of Wales inspects a composite regiment bound for the war in South Africa, 1899*

86 *(Overleaf) Afrikaner 'Amazons' prepare to defend Newcastle, Natal, at the outbreak of the Boer War in 1899*

87 *(Left) Edward, in German military uniform, stands one step away from the throne*

88 *Launching H.M.S.* Royal Sovereign *at Portsmouth in February 1891*

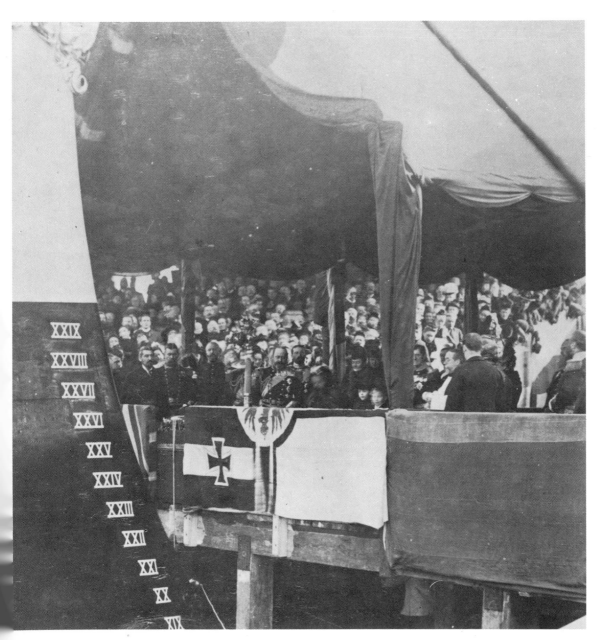

89–91 Edward's flamboyant nephew, the Kaiser Wilhelm II – aboard his imperial yacht Hohenzollern, *and posturing in the uniform of a Death's Head Hussar; the* Hohenzollern *illuminated at Cowes, 1895*

92 (Opposite, above) Three royal brothers, their whiskers turning white, photographed in 1894: (from left to right) Alfred of Saxe-Coburg, the Prince of Wales, the Duke of Connaught

93 (Opposite, below) Edward, with pickelhaube *uneasily tilted, stands with the Kaiser at the Military School of Marksmanship, Spandau, in March 1890*

94 Royal tour of the Duke of Connaught (fourth from the left) to India in the late 1880s

95 A boisterous reception for the Prince of Wales after his horse 'Persimmon' had won the Derby in 1896

96 (Left) The attempted assassination of Edward by a Belgian student anarchist in Brussels station, April 1900. Edward remained cool, and joked about the youth's bad marksmanship

97, 98 Edward, with Alexandra and her sister, the Dowager Tsarina of Russia, at the Danish Court in 1900. (Below) Alexandra greets her sister on the landing stage at Copenhagen

99 A German cartoon of 1901 (during the Boer War) mocks   100 (Right) Edward as a Freemason
Edward's extra-marital exploits. The caption reads, 'Aren't
you going to South Africa?' 'No, I must comfort the widows
and wives'

101, 102 (Opposite, above) Edward as Highland gentleman and portly warlord

104, 105 (Below) Edward in fancy dress for the Devonshire House Ball of 1897, and with pet dog and habitual cigar at Windsor

103 (Opposite, below) The Prince and Princess of Wales visit the great Liberal statesman Gladstone and his wife at Hawarden in May 1897, a year before the Grand Old Man's death

108 (Left) The Grand Old Man of late-Victorian politics, W. E. Gladstone, in noble pose

109 Queen Victoria's favourite Prime Minister, Benjamin Disraeli, later Earl of Beaconsfield

110 (Left) Four British monarchs: George V, Edward VII, Queen Victoria, and the infant Edward VIII in his christening gown

111 The future King Edward VIII, surrounded by Great-Grandmama, Grandpapa, and a still youthful Grandmama (Alexandra)

112 (Left) Princess Mary with two future monarchs, George VI and Edward VIII

113, 114 The Widow of Windsor

115 Four generations of British royalty

116 Print from a negative by James Reid, photographer of Ballater, near Balmoral. (Left to right) Princess Mary, the future Edward VIII, the future George VI, and doting Grandmama

117 (Opposite, above) Group at Balmoral. (Left to right) Princess Marie of Edinburgh, Princess Alexandra of Edinburgh, Princess Victoria of Edinburgh, the Duchess of Edinburgh, Queen Victoria, Princess Victoria of Prussia, Empress Frederick of Prussia, Princess Henry of Battenberg

118 (Opposite, below) Bizarre group at Balmoral, including a Highlander (not John Brown), Queen Victoria, and an Indian servant

119 (Below) Highland scenario, including the Tsar Nicholas II of Russia (second from the right)

120 (Below left) A rare photograph of Queen Victoria smiling, at Osborne, Isle of Wight, 1898

121 (Below right) Lower Regent Street decorations for Victoria's Diamond Jubilee in 1897

122 (Overleaf) Queen Victoria leaves St Paul's Cathedral after the Diamond Jubilee Thanksgiving Service

Chapter Three

King Edward, 1901

On 22 January 1901 Queen Victoria died at Osborne, surrounded by her family. On her death bed she had embraced the sobbing Prince of Wales and called out 'Bertie'; it was her last conscious word. A few hours later she died in the arms of her distraught grandson, the Kaiser, who had come post-haste from Germany to be near her. She had reigned for sixty-four years, longer than any other British monarch. An era had ended, and throughout Britain and the Empire millions of subjects were conscious of the fact that they could no longer call themselves 'Victorians'.

But, 'The Queen is dead. Long live the King!' The new sovereign attended the Accession Council at St James's Palace on 23 January where he adroitly jettisoned his first name of Albert and announced that he would be known as King Edward. He also spoke of the loss he and the nation had suffered through his mother's death and stated: 'My constant endeavour will be always to walk in her footsteps . . . I am fully determined to be a constitutional sovereign, in the strictest sense of the word, to work for the good and amelioration of my people.' After some discussion with the Unionist government, the Royal Style and Titles were amended in April 1901 and read: 'Edward VII, by the Grace of God, of Great Britain and Ireland, and of the British Dominions beyond the Seas, King, Defender of the Faith, Emperor of India.'

Edward's accession brought a gust of fresh air to the institution of monarchy. Even as he busied himself with the preparations for Queen Victoria's funeral, servants were beginning to spring-clean the royal residences. At Windsor, Eastern trophies were found infested with moths, and tons of rotting ivory were removed from an attic. In Buckingham Palace, so long untenanted by the old Queen, Albert's bizarrely preserved rooms were gutted, the plumbing was modernized and unacceptable paintings, furniture and bric-à-brac were carted off to be stored at Windsor Castle. Edward also decided to dispense with Osborne, which was eventually given to the Royal Navy for the training of cadets.

The stiff and gloomy court life of Victoria was also scrapped. Instead, Edward held glittering evening courts in the ballroom of Buckingham Palace, and ordered the playing of popular tunes rather than more sober music, thus causing his Assistant Private Secretary Frederick Ponsonby to note the spectacle of 'eminent men being knighted while comic songs were being played'. The King's intense love of colourful ceremony provoked a warm public response, and the gorgeous pageantry of his first State Opening of Parliament, when the peers were told to arrive in their finest carriages, fully robed, was widely appreciated. Edward insisted on opening Parliament in person (the first time this had happened since 1886) and on reading the Speech from the Throne himself. He later made a point of undertaking royal progresses through his kingdom in order to meet the people. The subdued, monochromatic shades of Victoria's widowhood were suddenly transformed into vibrant

123 King at last. Edward VII in his coronation robes

and arresting colour tones.

Not all observers welcomed the new style of monarchy. *The Times* delivered some cautionary words on Edward's accession, commenting that he had been 'importuned by temptation in its most seductive form', and though he had 'never failed in his duty to the throne and the nation . . . we shall not pretend that there is nothing in his long career which those who respect and admire him would wish otherwise'. Lord Esher, a close personal friend of the King, and a confidant of the influential, also regretted the passing of what he called the 'mystery and awe of the old Court'.

One mystery which Edward immediately dispensed with concerned his heir's access to state papers. Whereas Queen Victoria had jealously guarded her position as sovereign in this respect, the King was anxious that Prince George should be fully initiated into his duties when his time to succeed came. He therefore opened all official secrets to his son and strove to give him confidence and insight. There is no doubt that the conservative, rigid, and rather diffident new Prince of Wales benefited enormously from his father's encouragement and help in this field.

Edward made up his royal household chiefly from those who had served him as Prince of Wales. Francis Knollys became Private Secretary to the King, with Arthur Davidson and Frederick Ponsonby as his assistants; Sir Dighton Probyn became Keeper of the Privy Purse, though other officials and friends kept an eye on the sovereign's financial affairs – notably Knollys, Sir Ernest Cassel and the ubiquitous Lord Esher. In view of Edward's inexperience of state business, his Private Secretaries had a particularly important and delicate role to play. Part of their duties consisted of putting the King's often forthright and intemperate responses to a variety of matters into diplomatic language; they also guarded against any encroachments on the already reduced royal prerogatives, and brought to the King's attention any matters that warranted a statement or some other response. Edward made an enthusiastic start in tackling the desk work of a constitutional monarch, probably because the reading of dispatches and Cabinet papers was a novelty for him; but after the first few months of his reign his appetite for paper work diminished and signature by rubber stamp was not uncommon.

The King's appetite for food, however, remained as voracious as ever. He ate a hearty breakfast for much of his life, though the problems of overweight (in 1902 he measured forty-eight inches round both his chest *and* his waist) later encouraged him to have a light, continental, breakfast; even so, if he was due to undertake some physical exercise during the day, shooting for instance, he still fortified himself with a breakfast of poached egg, bacon, haddock and chicken or woodcock. His luncheon was usually a gargantuan affair, and included the game dishes of which he was extraordinarily fond, such as partridge or pheasant stuffed with snipe or woodcock which were in turn stuffed with truffles and the whole dish smothered with a rich sauce. His dinners rarely had less than twelve courses, one of which was invariably grilled oysters when in season; but his gastronomic tastes were completely comprehensive and ranged from roast beef and Yorkshire pudding to deer pie and quails *à la Grecque*. So eagerly did he eat whatever was put before him that his appetite appalled his wife, who called it 'terrible'; moreover, he bolted his food rather than chewing it properly.

He also drank champagne and claret, though in moderation. After dinner he enjoyed one glass of brandy, but, predictably, was eager to join the ladies, and did not linger over his

KING EDWARD HEARTILY BIDS YOU WELCOME TO HIS CORONATION DINNER, ON JULY 5TH. 1902.

124 *An invitation to the coronation dinner scheduled for 5 July 1902, but postponed due to the King's emergency operation for appendicitis on 24 June*

liqueurs. His addiction to tobacco, however, was excessive. Before breakfast he rationed himself to one small cigar and two cigarettes, but thereafter he smoked an average of twelve large cigars and twenty cigarettes every day. Though towards the end of his life he was troubled with bronchitis and respiratory difficulties, he did not cut down his smoking and failed to enjoy one of his large cigars only on the morning of his death.

Fortunately Edward's finances were able to take the strain of such lavish habits, and Francis Knollys was able to claim that 'for the first time in English history, the heir apparent comes forward to claim his right to the throne unencumbered by a single penny of debt.' But, in addition, a Select Committee of the House of Commons recommended a number of increases in the allowances paid to the new monarch and members of the royal family; Edward was allotted an annual income of £470,000 (compared with Victoria's £385,000), Queen Alexandra's income was also raised, and so was that of the Prince of Wales – to £90,000. The government also agreed to defray the cost of visits to Britain by foreign sovereigns, though in 1907 the Treasury unsuccessfully challenged this principle.

So, King at last, popular, well-financed, intensely active in both the public and the private spheres, it only remained for Edward to be crowned. The coronation was originally arranged for 26 June 1902. Early in June, however, the King developed appendicitis; at first he refused to contemplate postponing the ceremony, but on 23 June his doctors told him that he now had peritonitis which would kill him unless he straightway underwent an operation. Edward was still determined not to disappoint his subjects and argued furiously with his doctors until Sir Francis Laking gently persuaded him to agree to an operation the next day.

A special room was prepared at Buckingham Palace, and at 12.25 p.m. on 24 June the King underwent a forty-minute operation which, though then regarded as risky surgery, was completely successful. As he regained consciousness the King's first words were 'Where's George?' (the Prince of Wales), but an oversentimental press translated this into the poignant question, 'Will my people ever forgive me?' The nation was both shocked by the news of the King's operation and overjoyed by its successful outcome. As the news ran through the capital the Bishop of London hastily transformed the coronation dress-rehearsal into a service of intercession.

Most of the imperial and foreign dignitaries who had assembled in London for 26 June were obliged to return home before the postponed coronation took place on 9 August. Edward was fully recovered from his operation, bronzed from a convalescent cruise, and six inches less round the waist. Robed in splendour the King summoned his awe-struck grandchildren to see him before he set off for Westminster Abbey and, noting their be-musement, commented kindly, 'Good morning, children. Am I not a funny-looking old man?' Edward stood the abbreviated ceremony well, and was much moved when the Prince of Wales came to swear allegiance to him. The crowds were rapturous in their reception of him and of the radiantly beautiful Queen Alexandra, while better informed, or more cynical, observers inside the Abbey noted the special box, wryly nicknamed 'The King's Loose Box', which contained (among others) Sarah Bernhardt, Lady Kilmorey Mrs Arthur Paget, and the current favourite, Mrs George Keppel. The coronation, which was also marked by a £30,000 banquet given to the poor of London, was, in the event, a particularly British celebration: there were few foreign representatives, and the nation could be thankful that two months previously it had emerged from the harrowing and divisive years of the Boer War; moreover, there was now a monarch with whom, for all his love of high society, for all his expensive tastes, the people could identify. The robust reign of the 'runabout King' had begun in earnest.

125 The coronation procession passes down Whitehall

126 *The Throne Room at Buckingham Palace. Edward ordered that, on official occasions when he conferred knighthoods, light tunes should be played instead of the more solemn music of Queen Victoria's day*

127 *Edward taking the coronation oath*

128 *The King in full majesty. During the latter part of his
life Edward measured as much round the waist as round the
chest, and his friends privately called him 'Tum-tum'*

OUR CORONATION BO
GOD SAVE THE

CHILLINGTON,   VII

133 (Opposite, above) The picture gallery in Buckingham Palace. Edward had many of his mother's pictures removed

134 (Opposite, below) The White Drawing-room in Buckingham Palace

135 The royal chapel within Buckingham Palace. Queen Alexandra was a devout Christian, Edward less so

136 Edward in his study at Marlborough House. Despite the novelty of desk work he soon became bored by it

137 (Overleaf) The Ball and Concert Room at Buckingham Palace. Edward's reign was marked by sparkling receptions and sumptuous balls

138 Sir Ernest Cassel, Edward's financier friend. The King had close friendships with a number of Jewish financial experts

139 (Inset) Lord Esher, Edward's somewhat sycophantic confidant and a power behind the throne

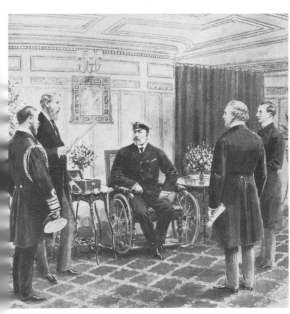

147 *A royal visit to Chatsworth in 1907. Edward's mistress Mrs George Keppel is on the extreme left, and his host the Duke of Devonshire stands at the King's left shoulder*

148 *(Below left) Edward in naval uniform. He was an indefatigable yachtsman and a staunch supporter of the dynamic Admiral Jacky Fisher*

149 *(Below right) A photograph captioned 'King Edward in private life'*

150 *(Right) Proud grandfather with Prince Edward, Prince George (Duke of Kent), Princess Mary (the Princess Royal) and Prince Albert (George VI) at Balmoral in 1902*

Chapter Four

His Majesty's Governments, 1901–10

King Edward's reign was neatly divided into a period of Unionist government (1901–5) and a period of Liberal government (1905–10). When Edward succeeded to the throne, Lord Salisbury's Unionist administration had been in power since 1895 and had recently seen its mandate renewed at the 'Khaki' election of 1900, during the Boer War. The ensuing decade was destined to be one of violent political controversy and substantial social reform; it also included a fundamental restructuring of Britain's foreign policy. It was an era of bitter industrial dispute, suffragette militancy, the protracted conflict between the House of Commons and the House of Lords (which ended in the 1911 Parliament Act), the naval armaments race with Germany, and the scrapping of 'splendid isolation'. Indeed, the Edwardian Age, far from being a sun-lit, unruffled prelude to the trauma and slaughter of the Great War, was a period of considerable disruption, conflict, and uncertainty. Writing in 1909, C. F. G. Masterman made the following observation: 'We can find no answer to the inquiry, whether we are about to plunge into a new period of tumult and upheaval, whether we are destined to an indefinite prolongation of the present half-lights and shadows, whether, as we sometimes try to anticipate, a door is about to be opened, revealing unimaginable glories.'

The King, being of a conservative disposition, might have been expected to cooperate admirably with his first, Unionist, government. The Unionists were an alliance of the Conservatives, the Liberal Unionists and a few Chamberlainite radicals; their Prime Minister was the Third Marquis of Salisbury. But, when Edward became King, Salisbury was within a year and a half of his retirement, and apt to doze off at Cabinet meetings; in 1901, during the Boer War, he was also reported to have picked up a photograph of the King and to have pensively remarked: 'Alas, poor Buller, what a mess he made of it.' At any rate, though the relationship between Salisbury and Edward was cordial enough, the ageing Prime Minister did not have the inclination to provide the new monarch with the tuition in state business that he so desperately needed.

Salisbury's successor as Prime Minister was his nephew Arthur James Balfour. Aloof, verbally dextrous, fastidious, and deeply interested in philosophy and the arts, Balfour had almost nothing in common with the King – not even a passion for women. Balfour, according to Henry Ponsonby, the late Queen's Private Secretary, had always been 'a great success with Victoria, although to me he never seemed to treat her seriously'; but with Edward he was far less of a success, and paid scant attention to royal opinion. The King, for his part, resented Balfour's 'slight courtesy' (as he once described it), and considered his Prime Minister to be 'always so vague'.

There were various sharp disagreements between Balfour and the King, some of them petty but some touching the prerogatives of the Crown. In 1902, for example, Edward

153 Edward dressed to review the Royal Navy. Naval defence was one of the crucial issues of his reign

154 (Overleaf) The Edwardian House of Commons: Balfour stands near the dispatch box

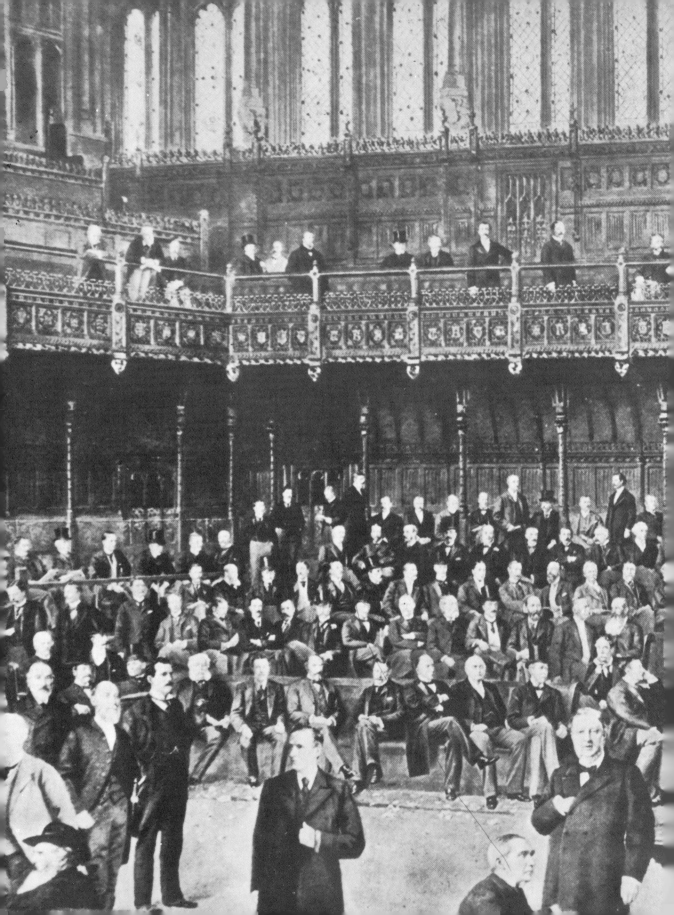

steadfastly refused to confer the Order of the Garter, which was in the Crown's gift, upon the visiting Shah of Persia, even though that potentate had been led to believe that he would receive the coveted honour; the King's attitude arose from his displeasure that the Foreign Office had failed to consult him over the matter. Edward was also critical of Balfour's handling of the Tariff Reform crisis in 1903; Joseph Chamberlain, the dynamic and charismatic Colonial Secretary, resigned from the Cabinet after proposing that Britain's Free Trade policy should be drastically altered, and four Free Trade ministers also resigned. The King resented the fact that Balfour released the names of the resigning ministers to the press without having seen him first; he also proposed that a Royal Commission should look into the whole Tariff Reform question, but the Prime Minister would not accept the proposal. Edward was further annoyed that the government did not consult him when it offered a funeral with military honours after the death of ex-President Kruger of the Transvaal.

Towards many of the domestic and colonial issues of the day the King showed little interest. The problems of defence and foreign policy, however, did concern him. He was particularly anxious that defence reforms should be forced through in the aftermath of the poorly-prosecuted Boer War. Through his close contact with Lord Esher, Edward kept a watchful eye on the work of various committees set up to overhaul military matters. He was also a firm supporter of Admiral Fisher's drive, as First Sea Lord, to carry through a sweeping reorganization of the Royal Navy and to build up the Dreadnought class of big-gunned battleship. Perhaps the King's admiration for Jackie Fisher owed something to the latter's ebullience and verve, and it was noticed that once when Fisher suggested rolling back the carpets at Buckingham Palace for an unscheduled dance, the King, who preferred court life to be well-ordered, readily agreed.

But it was in the field of foreign policy that Edward made his greatest popular impact. This was chiefly because the early years of his reign coincided with Britain shaking off her sometimes embarrassing reliance upon 'splendid isolation'. A limited Anglo-Japanese alliance was concluded in 1902, and in 1904 the *entente cordiale* resolved Anglo-French tension in a number of areas – notably Egypt, Morocco, Siam and West Africa. In 1903 King Edward had paid a royal visit to Paris which had been a singular personal and diplomatic triumph. No stranger to the delights of the French capital, the King had employed all his charm and tact to enchant the French crowds. But the *entente cordiale* did not spring unexpectedly out of this visit, which merely provided a climax to two years of diplomatic activity. Still, Edward could be an excellent ambassador, even though Balfour subsequently wrote disparagingly that 'he never made an important suggestion of any sort on large questions of policy'.

In December 1905 the Unionist government resigned, its following embarrassingly divided over the Tariff Reform issue. To the last, Balfour refused to take the King's advice seriously, and declined either to dissolve Parliament or to risk defeat in the Commons. The Unionist tactics were aimed at forcing the feuding Liberal leadership to take office in a state of disarray; in the event, the Liberal-Imperialist plot to kick the party leader Sir Henry Campbell-Bannerman 'upstairs' to the House of Lords failed, and the new Prime Minister was able to construct a Cabinet that represented the different factions in the party – the Liberal-Imperialists (on the right wing), the Gladstonian centre, and the radical Left.

The general election of January 1906 annihilated the Unionists, of whom only 157 were returned to the Commons. The Liberals had an overall majority of 84; since the government could, in most circumstances, count on the support of the Irish Nationalists and the infant Labour party, it could reckon on 513 votes against 157, a majority of 356.

What was the King to make of this electoral revolution? His son, the Prince of Wales, had already commented on the 53 Labour MPs, saying: 'I see that a great number of Labour members have been returned which is rather a dangerous sign, but I hope they are not all Socialists.' Surprisingly, Edward's relations with the new Liberal government were at first extremely cordial. The King had become acquainted with Campbell-Bannerman at Biarritz, and found him agreeable company, perhaps chiefly for his straightforward manner and for his interest in good food. Nor was Campbell-Bannerman's Cabinet particularly menacing, containing as it did a good ballast of Liberal-Imperialists, men like Asquith, Grey and Haldane, who were unlikely to desecrate the institution of monarchy.

Edward continued to cooperate well with Campbell-Bannerman, and was sorry to have to contemplate his resignation early in 1908 through ill-health, remarking: 'it would be a bad day for the country if anything happened to Campbell-Bannerman.' The Prime Minister did resign, however, and the King exercised his prerogative in sending for Asquith to replace him. Edward cared less for Asquith, whom he considered to be secretive and not prepared to be fully frank with him over government business. Certainly Asquith trimmed his regular written reports of Cabinet meetings to suit the King's interests, and perhaps also his prejudices. Some of Asquith's colleagues, moreover, actually antagonized Edward; he distrusted Lloyd George, who became Chancellor of the Exchequer in 1908, and also Asquith's Home Secretary, Winston Churchill, the lapsed Conservative turned fiery radical.

The King was generally an asset in the formation and prosecution of the Liberal government's foreign policy. His continental travels sometimes smoothed the path of the Foreign Office; he regularly called on the French President whenever he passed through Paris, and in 1907 had a fruitful meeting with Georges Clemenceau at Marienbad. He actively aided the discussions resulting in the Anglo-Russian *entente* of 1907, and when earlier he visited Vienna the journal *Die Zeit* noted that 'The Englishman is free and without fear of his King and the King is free and . . . . . not afraid of the Viennese'. Other monarchs probably overestimated Edward's statesmanship, and the Kaiser concluded that the King was 'a Satan, you can hardly believe what a Satan he is'. The press also at times exaggerated his influence, and there was one caption to a photograph showing Edward and Campbell-Bannerman in Marienbad which read 'Is it peace or war?' In fact, as Campbell-Bannerman later disclosed, they had merely been discussing whether halibut was better baked or boiled.

Over domestic policy, however, the King found himself more and more at odds with the Liberals. He resolutely opposed women's suffrage, and disliked the government's proposal to legalize peaceful picketing during industrial disputes. He also strongly objected to certain public statements by the more radical members of the Cabinet – like Lloyd George. But in particular he was deeply disturbed by the growing conflict between the government and the Conservative-dominated House of Lords. The Lords began to block reforming Liberal measures, and in 1909 precipitated a serious constitutional crisis by rejecting Lloyd George's provocative 'People's Budget'. In January 1910 the general election returned the Liberals to power, but with a much reduced majority, thus making them dependent in the Commons upon Irish Nationalist and Labour support. Asquith now introduced a Parliament Bill aimed at reducing the delaying powers of the House of Lords, and asked the King for a guarantee that if the Lords rejected this Bill he would create sufficient Liberal peers to vote it through. Edward, disliking the political and constitutional implications of this request, refused it.

Before the crisis could move to its climax, however, the King died. On 4 May 1910, his son noted in his diary: 'Saw Papa; his colour was bad and his breathing fast.' The King was, in fact, struggling with a serious attack of bronchitis. On 6 May he ate a light lunch and then suffered a series of heart attacks. As he lost his grip on life, the Prince of Wales was able to tell him that his horse 'Witch of the Air' had won that afternoon at Kempton Park; appropriately, it was virtually the last news that he heard. That evening, at 11.45, he died, and the new King, George V, recorded in his diary, 'I have lost my best friend and the best of fathers. I never had a word with him in my life. I am heartbroken and overwhelmed with grief.'

155 *The third Marquis of Salisbury, Edward's first Prime Minister*

156 *Arthur James Balfour, Unionist Prime Minister 1902–5. Aloof and intellectually agile, he treated Edward with scant respect and was cordially disliked in return*

157 *Sir Henry Campbell-Bannerman, Liberal Prime Minister 1905–8. Edward had earlier met C-B at Biarritz and thought highly of him*

158 *Asquith, Liberal Prime Minister 1908–16. The King found him too secretive and less than frank*

159 *(Right) The great dynamic force of early Edwardian politics, Joseph Chamberlain (Colonial Secretary 1895–1903, and tariff reformer), with his third wife*

160 (Left) Two radical Liberals distrusted by King Edward, David Lloyd George and Winston Churchill – the latter having recently discovered the poor

162 Cecil John Rhodes, diamond magnate and imperial expansionist. Though Rhodes was a 'woman hater', Edward admired him as a 'man of action'

161 President Kruger of the Transvaal, arch-opponent of the bid to establish British supremacy in South Africa

163 Edward's nephew-by-marriage, the Tsar Nicholas II, who bore a remarkable resemblance to the King's own son Prince George

164 A suffragette, Mrs Drummond, addresses a predominantly male audience in Trafalgar Square. Edward did not approve of 'votes for women', although he strongly approved of women

166 (Above) A postcard issued to celebrate the Anglo-French entente of 1904

167 (Below) Edward is greeted in Paris on his famous diplomatic mission of 1903 to help prepare the entente cordiale

168 *Edward goes racing in Paris. In this contemporary
drawing he is inspecting the famous stallion 'Renard Volant'
('Flying Fox')*

169 *Edward and the French President, M. Fallières, at the Franco-British Exhibition in Paris*

170 *The King plants the* entente cordiale *tree in the grounds of the British Embassy in Paris*

171, 172 *Edward relaxing at the races at St Cloud in 1905, and later leaving by car*

173 *(Right) At the fashionable spa of Marienbad, taking 'the cure' of the famous mineral waters*

174 Edward sitting with an apparently grumpy Shah of
Persia on whom he refused to confer the Order of the Garter in
1902

176 (Right) Which twin is the Tsar? The cousins Nicholas
II (left) and the Prince of Wales at Cowes in 1904

175 (Below) A mingling of the inter-related British, Russian
and Danish royal houses

177, 178 *Relaxed uncle and strident nephew (the Kaiser Wilhelm II) at Berlin in 1909; the Kaiser shares a joke with the Austrian military attaché during army manoeuvres in Germany*

179 *(Right) The Kaiser with his uncles Edward and the Duke of Connaught at Windsor in 1907*

180 *King Edward inspecting the army at Aldershot*

181 *(Below) Edward touches the colours in an act of temporal consecration at Aldershot, 1909*

182 *(Right) Edward as host to the Queen of Portugal. The Portuguese monarchy was overthrown in 1910 four months after Edward's death*

Chapter Five

Epilogue: Edward and his Times

King Edward's death had been sudden and therefore unexpected. John Morley, Secretary of State for India, wrote: 'The feeling of grief and the sense of personal loss throughout the country, indeed throughout Western Europe, is extraordinary. It is in a way deeper and keener than when Queen Victoria died . . . more personal. He had just the character that Englishmen, at any rate, thoroughly understand, thoroughly like . . . . He combined regal dignity with *bonhomie*, and strict regard for form with entire absence of spurious pomp.' Queen Alexandra confessed that 'she had been turned into stone, unable to cry, unable to grasp the meaning of it all, and incapable of doing anything'.

As the dead King's body lay in state in Westminster Hall a quarter of a million people passed by to pay their respects, and Halley's comet blazed portentously in the night skies. On 20 May the funeral procession wound through the London streets watched by huge crowds. Foreign royalty and dignitaries attended the funeral ceremonies, among them the Kaiser, the Kings of Belgium, Bulgaria, Denmark, Greece, Norway, Portugal and Spain, the Archduke Franz Ferdinand of Austria-Hungry and the Dowager Empress of Russia.

What was the secret of Edward's appeal? At one level, of course, he was a symbol of security in uncertain times; he linked the halcyon years of the Great Exhibition with Britain's more troubled economic prospects in the early twentieth century; Lord Palmerston had concerned himself with his marriage prospects, Winston Churchill had perturbed his later years; when he had been born the vast majority of British males had been unenfranchised, when he died women were clamouring for the vote; for much of his life the Royal Navy had effortlessly ruled the waves, yet in his last years the German naval challenge had proved a source of grave anxiety.

A further explanation of his popularity has been offered in George Dangerfield's book *The Strange Death of Liberal England*, where the author suggests that Edward 'represented in a concentrated shape those bourgeois Kings whose florid forms and rather dubious escapades were all the industrialized world had left of an ancient divinity; his people saw in him the personification of something nameless, genial and phallic.'

Certainly Edward's nine years as King strengthened his appeal to his people. He was, at the very least, visible to his subjects, and travelled more widely and with more gusto than any British monarch for centuries (indeed he was the first sovereign to visit the Isle of Man since King Canute). His year began with the State Opening of Parliament, then in the spring he left for Biarritz, via Paris; in April he and his Queen dutifully visited the Danish court, but soon there was the English summer and Derby week and Royal Ascot; in July and August Edward was entertained by his aristocratic and wealthy friends, and attended Cowes Regatta; in the early autumn he travelled to Marienbad for 'the cure' of mineral water; later on, there was shooting at Balmoral, and finally Christmas at Windsor

83 Lord Montagu of Beaulieu about to take Edward for a
in in a 12-h.p. Daimler in 1899

or Sandringham. During his comparatively brief stays in London he entertained at Buckingham Palace and Marlborough House.

Entertaining the King was not always as easy as Hilaire Belloc imagined in a ballad composed for private circulation:

> *There will be bridge and booze 'til after three,*
> *And, after that, a lot of them will grope*
> *Along the corridors in* robes de nuit,
> *Pyjamas, or some other kind of dope.*
>
> *A sturdy matron will be set to cope*
> *With Lord _____ , who isn't 'quite the thing',*
> *And give his wife the leisure to elope,*
> *And Mrs. James will entertain the King!*

In fact, Edward was notoriously easily bored, and could vent his wrath upon, or icily snub, those whom he found irksome. His restlessness was partly the expression of his incapacity for calm introspection, and of his lack of absorbing intellectual and cultural tastes. Practical jokes, racy chat and witty remarks, however, could keep him amused, though far too often his hosts realized with dread that he was once more drumming his fingers on the table and murmuring ominously 'Quite so, quite so'.

Hunting was one way of keeping the King occupied, though he preferred game to be driven before his guns rather than stalking it. Edward slaughtered thousands of wild animals and birds during his lifetime, and among the creatures he bagged were tigers, bears, crocodiles, elks, chamois, deer, wild boar, rabbits, partridges and pheasants. Competitive games were more of a problem. Edward disliked being beaten whether at cards, croquet or golf. His passion for the latter sport was considerable, despite his portly figure, though he often demanded that bunkers into which he inadvertently hit balls should be moved within the next twenty-four hours!

The King's enthusiasm for horse-racing was a quality that endeared him to many of his subjects – though perhaps not to radicals and Nonconformists. He loved the jostle and excitement of race meetings, and was overjoyed when his horse 'Minoru' won the Derby in 1906 and the spectators called out 'Good Old Teddy' and sang 'God Save the King'. He also became a keen motorist, purchasing expensive vehicles and insisting that they should be painted claret and not carry number plates. He once broke the speed-limit by driving at 60 mph along the Brighton Road, and also enjoyed taking a car up difficult mountain tracks.

He still pursued, and was pursued by, women. Foreign beauties offered themselves at Marienbad or Homburg, or met the King discreetly at Paris or Copenhagen. No doubt some of the gossip exceeded the facts, and, because of his reputation, some women to whom he had merely been civil imagined that he was importuning them. Nonetheless, Edward's activities in the boudoir were apparently unimpaired by his advancing years and were perhaps appropriate enough in an era that was beginning to slough off the more stifling moral conventions of Victorian society.

Edward was, of course, a confirmed snob in the sense that he never questioned his right to social pre-eminence. He unashamedly enjoyed the company of the wealthy and the high-born, and resented those who threatened to break down class barriers or upset

158

184, 185 *The King, prudently wearing goggles, sets off in 1906 for a day at the races in his car. His cars were painted claret, and bore no numbers. A most enthusiastic motorist, he once drove along the Brighton Road at a dizzy (and illegal) 60 m.p.h.*

186 *(Below) Jolly boating weather. The royal party take an up-river trip*

the social structure. Yet he rarely went out of his way to make people feel uncomfortable, though once he told the Duchess of Rutland that she did not brush her hair! Generally he was tactful, as when he noticed that a visiting Indian prince was throwing his asparagus stalks on to the floor at Buckingham Palace, and promptly began throwing his own down too.

His ability to comprehend the powerful forces at work within Edwardian, and world, society was sadly limited. When shown how the London poor lived, his first instinct was to scatter handfuls of sovereigns among them; it did not seem to occur to him that the left-wing Liberals and the Labour men, of whom he fundamentally disapproved, were proposing to take some practical steps to counteract poverty. He objected when Labour MPs described his 1908 meeting with the Tsar at Reval as 'hob-nobbing with blood-stained monsters', and straightway banned Keir Hardie and two other socialists from a royal garden party. Irish nationalism, the early activities of the Indian Congress movement, European Communism and syndicalism were equally unwelcome expressions of forces that were inexorably altering a world once dominated by the Pax Britannica and the industrial prowess of Lancashire and Birmingham.

Though in many ways Edward hankered for the past, he lived robustly in the present. It was, naturally enough, a present which he strove to make as congenial as possible. His upbringing had been stultifying and over-ambitious, but he had in the last resort managed to set his own standards and follow his own course. There was a great deal in his life that was trivial, superficial and self-indulgent. Nor was he particularly able or gifted. He was, however, vigorous, straightforward and marvellously alive. Moreover he brought to his public duties that zest and flamboyance that marked so much of his private life. He was, within his own terms, a good husband, a devoted father, and a conscientious sovereign, and when he died he left the British monarchy more popular and more secure than when he ascended the throne.

187, 188 Piccadilly Circus, with flower-sellers but without neon advertisements; and Piccadilly at the start of the Edwardian era

189 (Opposite, above) *Park Lane, comparatively deserted*

190 (Opposite, below) *Brompton Road, with Harrods Store, in 1905*

191 *Delectable and spotless Edwardian ladies at a 1903 garden party*

192 *Less fortunate females working at trouser finishing in 1906*

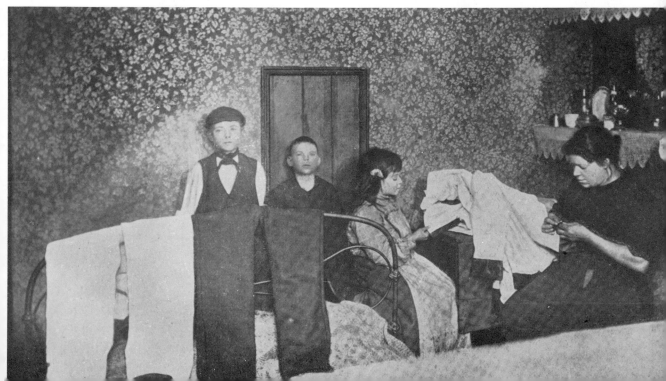

193 (Left) A suffragette procession about to move off, led by Mrs Drummond on horseback

194 Windows at Holloway prison shattered by militant suffragettes

198 *Slum houses in Westminster, within a stone's throw of the 'Mother of Parliaments'*

199 *(Right) A London flower-seller – shades of Eliza Doolittle*

202 (Far left) A model golfer of 1907; note the embryo plus-fours

203 (Left) Edward dressed to kill

204 (Below left) Dartmouth naval cadets organize a race with assorted competitors

205, 206 Edward shooting at Sandringham. Though a keen huntsman, the King came to prefer his game driven conveniently towards him

207 (Overleaf) Time for a break during a shooting party at Sandringham

208 *Prince George was a far better shot than his Papa*

210, 211 *(Opposite) 'Good old Teddy' in his element at Epsom. The Prince of Wales (right of centre in top picture) looks less enraptured*

209 *A rest before the slaughter*

MISS TURNER FARLEY.

LT. COL. A. HICKMAN-MORGAN D.S.O.

MRS. HICKMAN-MORGAN

THE HON. MRS GEORGE KEPPEL

THE HON. GERALD PAGET

MRS GEORGE JOHNSTONE

THE EARL OF DUNRAVEN

*214 Russian boys from the Tsar's imperial yacht at Cowes
wave appropriate flags*

215 *Maxine Elliott, the American actress, manages to sit at Edward's side at Marienbad in 1909*

216 *(Overleaf) Edward braves the breezes of Biarritz*

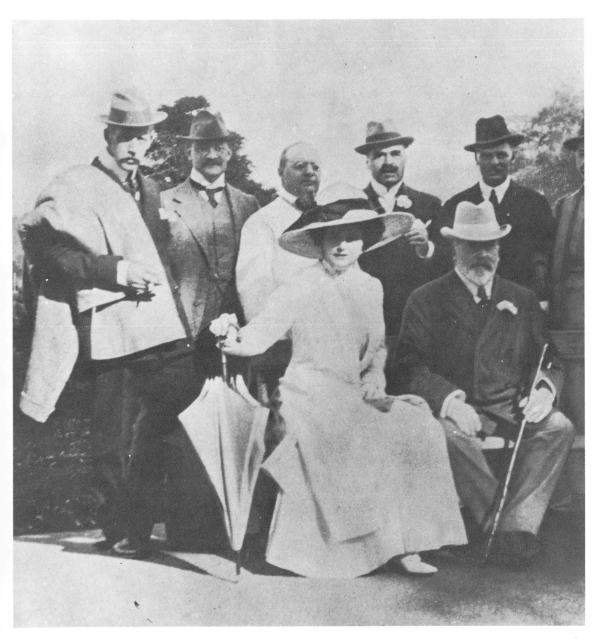

217 *The King and Queen land at Ramsey pier in 1902.*
Edward was the first monarch to visit the Isle of Man since
King Canute

218 *(Right) Edward visits the Duke of York's Military*
School, Chelsea, on Empire Day 1908, accompanied by
Queen Alexandra and (behind her) Princess Mary (the
future Queen Mary)

219, 220 (Opposite) The King and Queen open the new
Manchester Infirmary, and (below) the Royal Horticultural
Society's new hall in Vincent Square, Westminster

221 Edward at the opening of Birmingham's new water
supply from the great reservoir at Rhayader in 1904

222 (Left) The King and the Duke of Devonshire confront sheep and attendants at the 1906 Royal Agricultural Show at Derby

223 The Prince on the Clapham omnibus. The Prince of Wales at the inauguration of the first section of the L.C.C.'s electric tramways in 1903

224 Dame Nellie Melba, the great Australian soprano, who was at the height of her career during the Edwardian age

225 Edward at a lighter musical entertainment, Frocks and Frills, *at the Haymarket Theatre in 1902*

226 (Right) One of the greatest stars of the music halls that Edward enjoyed so much: buck-toothed, saucy, incomparable Marie Lloyd in 1905

> First Photograph
> ever telegraphed
> from Paris to
> — London. —
> November 7ᵗʰ, 1907.

"*The Daily Mirror,*"

12, Whitefriars Street,

Fleet Street, E.C.

The Editor of "The Daily Mirror" presents his compliments to

W. Martin-Hurst Eq

*and requests the pleasure of _____ his _____ company at the above offices
on Thursday evening, November 7th, at 9 o'clock, to witness a demonstration
and illustrated lecture by Professor KORN, of Munich University, of his
Telephotographic Apparatus, which has been installed by "The Daily Mirror,"
and which will transmit photographs between London and Paris. The favour
of an early reply will greatly oblige. Buffet 8 to 10.*

230 *A photograph taken by Edward's grandson, the future Edward VIII*

231 *Colonel of the Danish 1st Hussars*

232 *(Right) Bencher of the Middle Temple*

234,235 Edward and Alexandra on board the royal yacht at Cowes in 1902 (left) and 1905 (right). Edward seldom failed to attend the Cowes regatta, where he often met members of other European royal houses

195

236 *Alexandra, with dogs on the royal yacht, 1904*

237 *A slightly perplexed Alexandra (she was by now rather deaf) at the Temple Flower Show of 1909*

238, 239 *Edward in assorted headgear*

240 *(Above right)* *Three Kings in a row, George V,*
Edward VIII, Edward VII

241 *(Below right)* *Prince George, distressed at having to part*
from his parents, about to embark on S.S. Ophir in 1901 for
an eight-month royal progress round the far-flung Empire

242–5 *(Next pages) Journey's end: Queen Alexandra pays a*
last tribute to her dead husband on 7 May 1910; the King's
body lying in state in the Throne Room of Buckingham
Palace; foreign dignitaries, including the Kaiser (far left),
accompany the funeral cortège to Paddington Station for the
journey to Windsor; Edward's funeral procession, headed by
George V and eight sovereigns

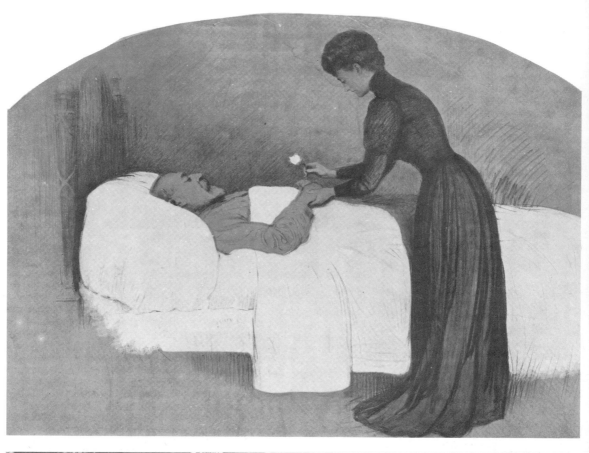

247 A closer view of the late King's horse and his favourite
terrier 'Caesar'

248 (Overleaf) 'The King is dead! Long live the King!'
George V on Epsom Downs, accompanied by a flurry of young
subjects, 1911

Select Bibliography

Benson, E. F.	*King Edward VII* (1933)
Cowles, V.	*Edward VII and His Circle* (1956)
Dangerfield, G.	*Victoria's Heir* (1942)
Dangerfield, G.	*The Strange Death of Liberal England* (1935)
Esher, Lord	*The Influence of King Edward* (1915)
Hearnshaw, P. (ed.)	*Edwardian England* (1933)
Judd, D.	*George V* (1973)
Lee, Sir S.	*King Edward VII* (2 vols.) (1925–7)
Longford, E.	*Victoria R.I.* (1964)
Magnus, Sir P.	*King Edward VII* (1964)
Maurois, A.	*Edward VII and His Times* (1933)
Middlemas, K.	*Edward VII* (1972)
Munz, S.	*King Edward VII at Marienbad* (1934)
Nicolson, Sir H.	*George V* (1952)
Nowell-Smith, S. (ed.)	*Edwardian England* (1964)
Ponsonby, Sir F.	*Recollections of Three Reigns* (1951)
Pope-Hennessy, J.	*Queen Mary* (1959)
Priestley, J. B.	*The Edwardians* (1970)
Read, D.	*Edwardian England* (1972)
Sackville-West, V.	*The Edwardians* (1935)
Tuchman, B.	*The Proud Tower* (1966)
Wortham, H. E.	*King Edward VII* (1933)